MUSICAL INSTRUMENTS
in
art

There are 12 Volumes in

Fine Art Books for Young People

We specialize in producing quality books for young people. For a complete list please write

LERNER PUBLICATIONS COMPANY
241 First Avenue North, Minneapolis, Minnesota 55401

MUSICAL
INSTRUMENTS
in
art

By Donald Celender, Ph.D, Designed by Wendell Carroll ■ Lerner Publications Company, Minneapolis, Minnesota.
Prepared under the supervision of Sharon Lerner, Art Editor

Second Printing 1967

The Musicians by Michelangelo Merisi da Caravaggio (1573-1610); The Metropolitan Museum of Art, Rogers Fund.

Contents

Introduction

Music has always been closely related to art. Man expresses his innermost feelings by either making sounds or drawing pictures. These arts are not only the means of personal expression. They were important in man's religious worship, too. Although this aspect is not so important today, we continue to use and combine music and the visual arts. Our modern purpose is to make our world a more enjoyable one.

Musical instruments have been a part of every ancient civilization. They are one of man's earliest inventions. We shall see that Egyptian slaves played instruments before the Pharaoh. Greek musicians produced music for social functions. Troubadours serenaded the kings and queens of Europe during the 16th and 17th centuries.

Musical instruments can be divided into three major groups: wind instruments, which make sound when air is blown into or across them; percussion instruments, which create sound when struck; and string instruments, in which a stretched string sets sound in motion.

The oldest of all instruments are those of the percussion group. These include the numerous types of drums used by all primitive peoples. Other members of the percussion group are tambourines, which were used by the Hebrews and Romans, the triangle, cymbals, gong, rattle and castenets. They are all based upon ancient examples.

Stringed instruments are the most numerous and are considered the most important in the modern orchestra. The wind and percussion instruments rely upon stringed instruments to serve as the foundation upon which the orchestra is built.

In ancient times, people learned to make melodic sounds by plucking stretched strings with either their hands or a small object called a *plectrum.* Their earliest stringed instrument was the harp, which has been played in all the ancient civilizations. One of the most popular harp-like instruments, the lyre, has often been pictured in Sumerian, Assyrian and Greek art.

The lute is somewhat similar to the harp and lyre. The guitar and banjo, two very popular stringed instruments today, are probable offshoots of the lute.

The piano is also a stringed instrument, with a long history. Its forerunner was a popular instrument of the Middle Ages called a dulcimer, which was played by plucking rather than hammering its strings.

The final group of stringed instruments are those which make sound vibrations by drawing a bow across the stretched strings. This group consists of the violin, viola, violoncello and the double-bass.

We have briefly reviewed the wide variety of musical instruments. Now we shall take a journey through the ages to see how artists from different cultures and times depicted them.

Flutist (20th Century), Israeli; Lerner Collection, Minneapolis.

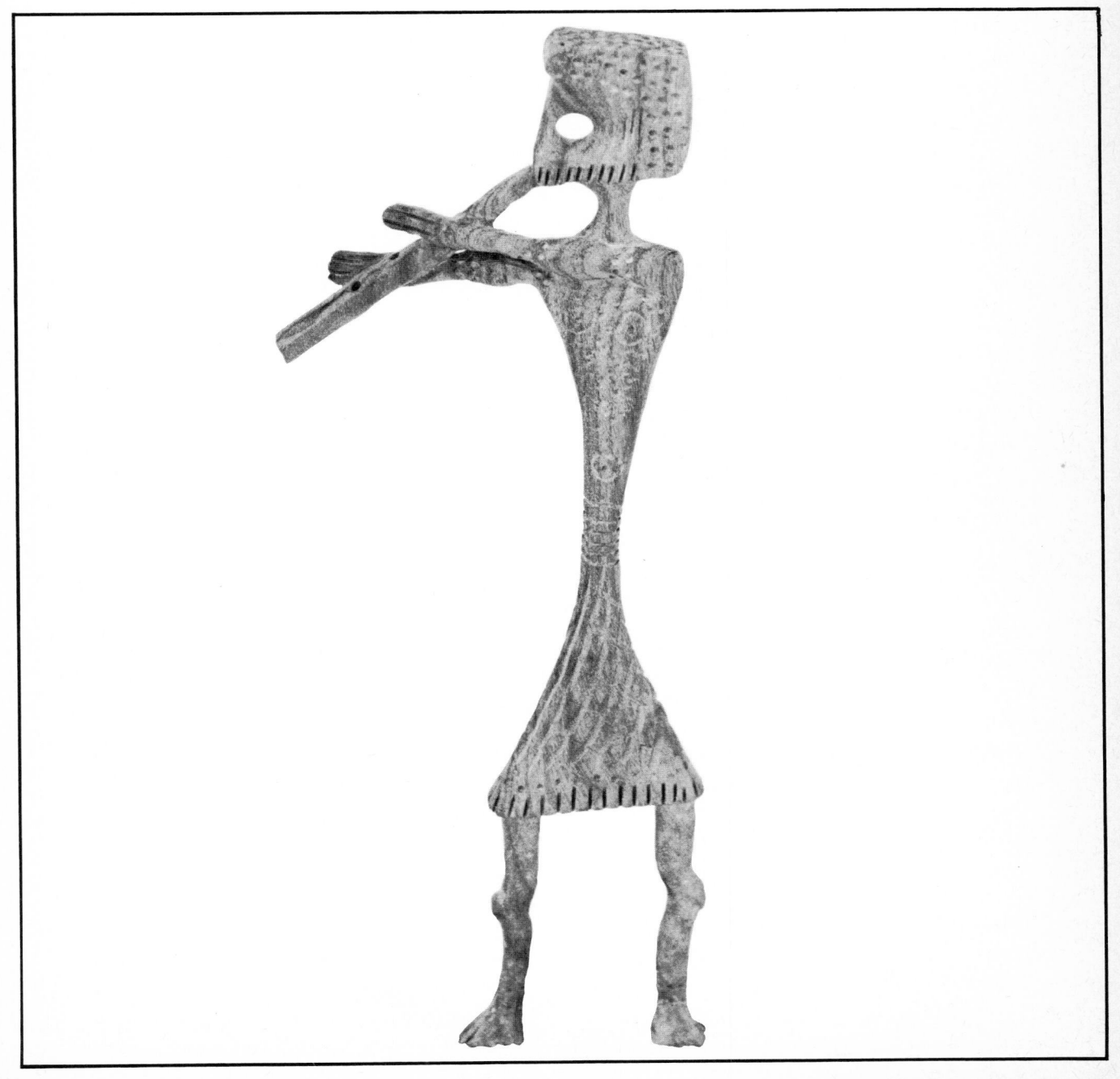

The Ancient World

Unfortunately, we shall never know the sound and character of music at the beginning of history. Much of our knowledge of early instruments is gained from sculptures, paintings, frescos, inlays, mosaics, and reliefs. Perhaps the most noteworthy musical objects of early times are those found in the region of the Tigres and Euphrates Rivers. These musical instruments were made by the Sumerians, an ancient civilization which settled in southern Mesopotamia, in what is present-day Iraq, Syria and Turkey, sometime before 4,000 B.C.

Among the Sumerians, as with many other ancient peoples, it was customary to fill the tomb or grave of a king or queen with household items, food, weapons and jewelry so

Harp of Queen Shub'Ad (c. 2600 B.C.), Sumerian; The University Museum, Philadelphia.

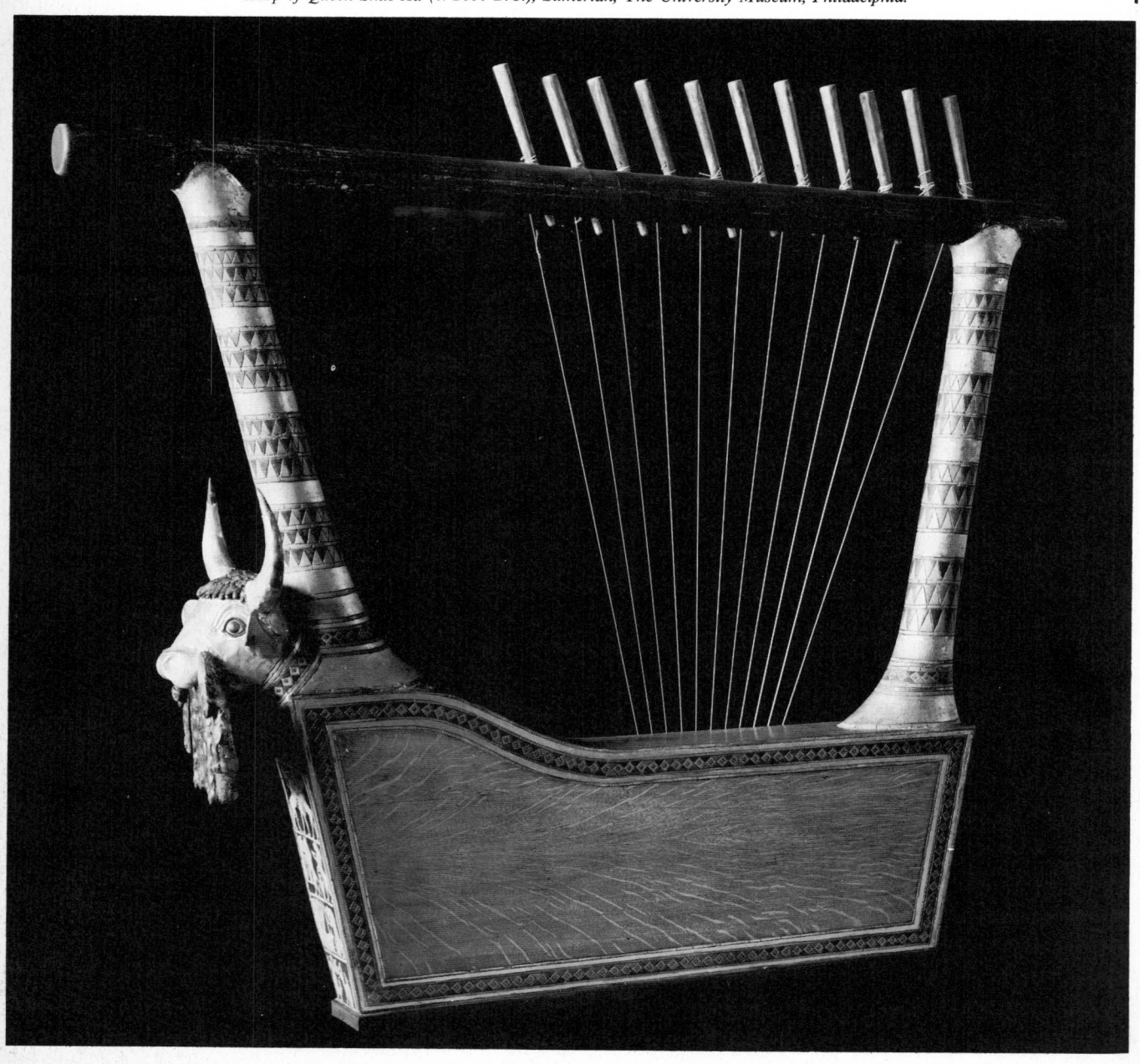

that the deceased would be comfortable in the world beyond. Archaeologists have uncovered a number of these objects.

This harp—*The Harp of Queen Shub'Ad*—was found in her tomb in Ur, an ancient Sumerian city. The harp is made of wood and covered with carved shell and gold. Its details, including the geometric designs and bull's head, are made of *lapis lazuli,* a precious blue mineral.

We can study the design on the soundbox. A soundbox is necessary because it increases the sound made by the plucked strings. This one has been decorated with people and animals. The person in the top compartment holding two bulls with human heads is Gilgamesh, a Sumerian hero. His placement in the center of the design tells us about the Sumerian's love for balance in art.

The sections below show animals doing a number of human jobs. A wolf and a lion carry food and drink to an unseen party. A donkey plucks a harp whose soundbox is being beaten by a bear. We can also see a deer strumming a small lyre. All of the animals are happily engaged in making music. In the bottom compartment of the soundbox a man, who looks like an insect, and a goat, carry objects taken from a large vase.

This amusing series of events is an example of *inlay* work. In this technique one type of material is set into another. Inlays of ivory, shell or colored stones occur often in Sumerian art.

Music was considered a gift given by the gods to the Sumerians. They believed that music could cure illnesses. They also thought that music could help a person live a happy and prosperous life. For these reasons, musicians were often pictured in the art of this period.

Inlay on Soundbox of Harp of Queen Shub'Ad

Flutist and Harpist (c. 2000 B.C.), Cycladic; National Museum, Athens.

These strikingly modern looking sculptural forms were carved almost 4,000 years ago. They represent two musicians, a flutist and a harpist. Little is known about the civilization that produced them.

Between 2600 and 100 B.C. a people called the Cycladics lived on a scattered group of small islands north of Crete in the Aegean Sea. They disappeared about 100 B.C., and left very little of their civilization for us to study. Only a few small tombs remain. The harpist and flutist were found in one of these burial places. Carved from marble, they are characteristic of the large number of religious statues fashioned by the Cycladic sculptors.

In general, these figures have flat, wedge-shaped bodies, column-like necks, and tilted, shield-shaped faces. The faces are featureless with the exception of long, ridge-like noses. Sizes of the statues vary from a few inches to life-sized figures. The best of them, such as our musicians, have a beautiful perfection which is beyond the range of other ancient art produced during this period.

We can only guess about the importance of music in the Cycladic culture. Apparently this early civilization had developed an intense love for music. A large number of musician sculptures are found in Cycladic tombs.

Musicians at a Banquet (1475-1448 B.C.), Egyptian; Thebes, Tomb of Amenemhet Tuthmosis III.

When we think of the huge pyramids in the vast deserts of Egypt, their size and mystery puzzle us. As they stand alone, surrounded by stretches of hot sand, they are not being seen as the Egyptians wanted them to be seen. In earlier times, pyramids were part of large groups of temples and buildings. Great religious parades were celebrated in these areas during the lifetimes of the Pharoahs who built them, as well as after their deaths. Music was an important part of the pageants. Practically all the walls of the tomb within a pyramid were covered with reliefs and paintings. Many of these, like our example, were scenes of musicians and dancers entertaining the Pharaoh and his guests. Such works were included in the tombs in order to help the person buried in the pyramid live happily in the next world. The Egyptians, like the Sumerians, believed their rulers were gods. After the rulers died, the Egyptians thought they would travel to another world and to the gods who had sent them to earth.

You may have noticed that Egyptian artists represented the human figure quite differently than artists do today. For the Egyptian, everything in life had to be represented from its most common angle. For example, a person's head was most easily represented in profile; therefore, the artist drew it in this manner. Since we think of the human eye as seen from the front, the artist always placed a front-view eye on a profile face. Next, the shoulders and chest are best seen from the front. Therefore, they, too, have to be rendered in this manner. But the arms, legs, and feet are most easily understood when seen in a side-view. Hence, the artist drew them accordingly. The final result is a human figure having some parts of its body shown from one angle, while other sections are portrayed from another. No person could exist this way in real life because our bodies are not capable of twisting to the extremes of our dancer and lyre player. Nevertheless, this is still a beautiful work of art which will continue to delight art lovers in future centuries as it has in the past.

Four Musicians (700 B.C.), Assyrian; Louvre, Paris, Photograph Giraudon.

The Assyrians were a warlike, powerful race. They lived in the same region, Mesopotamia, as the Sumerians. Although the Assyrians took control of the region about the 13th century B.C., they were not newcomers to the area. After coming to power, their rule lasted for many centuries. A tablet found there lists 107 Assyrian Kings.

Whenever the Assyrians conquered Mesopotamia, they adopted the culture and art of the area without changing them. The Sumerians left instruments such as cymbals, flutes, harps, lutes and lyres. These were further developed by the Assyrians.

In Assyria, music was an important part of religious worship. But it was used for everyday purposes as well. Several *reliefs*, or shallow carvings, have been found which show musicians performing for the king in his private gardens, for banquets and for military celebrations.

At the beginning of the seventh century the Assyrians played music during battle. This was done to help the soldiers fight better. The idea of our present day military bands goes back to the time of the Assyrians.

How do we know the Assyrian soldiers had music while they fought? Our relief shows us four battle musicians. They are facing each other two by two. Two men on one side are playing a *tabor,* or small drum with one head, and a five-stringed lyre. The other two musicians accompany them with cymbals and another lyre.

Assyrian artists were kept very busy by the king. He ordered them to cover the walls of his palace with hundreds of reliefs showing his power and the conquests of his army. The battles were described in minute detail, with both words and pictures carved into stone. These great *friezes* (freezes) represent one of the earliest large-scale attempts to show in art a series of events to inform a people.

Despite low carving, which makes the figures look flat, the forms of the four musicians seem solid. Assyrian carvers were very skillful artists. Stone was their favorite material. Because it is so hard and lasts such a long time we are able to study the life and times of an ancient people who lived over 2,500 years ago.

Greek painting is often forgotten when we study the art of this great ancient culture. The reason is simple; temples and statues still stand in Greece today, but paintings which once decorated the walls of temples and houses no longer exist. Only ancient writings tell us of these magnificent works.

However, a good understanding of Greek painting is available through the study of hundreds of painted vases which have survived the centuries. Many of these vase paintings are extremely beautiful and graceful, such as this one of a music lesson by the artist Phintias. The vase paintings, however, are much simpler than the large wall decorations described in ancient texts.

Many vase paintings depict musical scenes, and with good reason. Music had a special place in Greek life. It was a part of every phase of daily life, accompanying schoolchildren in classes of poetry and mathematics, workers in the fields, shopkeepers in the markets, and soldiers in battle. Festivals and social gatherings provided still more outlets for the Greek musician, who occupied a respected position in Greek society.

Unlike other highly developed art forms of Greek culture, the majority of instruments were simple and somewhat primitive. The lyre, shown twice in this vase painting, was the most popular instrument of ancient Greece. Perhaps this can be explained by the fact that it was easily played.

The Music Lesson (c. 510 B.C.), Greek; Staatliche Antikersammlungen, Munich.

The Etruscans were a people who lived about 2,800 years ago. Their origins are obscure, but they may have come from the area now called Turkey and Syria. Ancient legend claims they migrated to Italy because of famine in their homeland. The best source of information on Etruscan life comes from their burial places. They often built tombs to resemble houses. These burial chambers, although carved out of rock, had imitation wooden beams, and were filled with the utensils of daily life, furniture, clothing, ornaments, and painting and sculpture. The Etruscans were conquered by the Romans and disappeared as a separate nation.

Musicians and dancers in beautifully colored clothes weave in and out of the lavish banquet tables in several Etruscan tomb *frescos.* Frescos are wall paintings made with water colors on freshly applied, moist plaster.

Our example is part of a banquet scene painted on the back wall of the tomb. Dancers and musicians are shown on the other walls, too. In this fresco one young boy hurries ahead with a large bowl in his hand, another blows a double flute, while a third plucks the strings of a lyre. The music being made thrills not only the guests, but the musicians as well.

The Etruscans thought music was necessary in every part of their daily lives. They liked the double flute best of all the musical instruments. It is shown in this fresco, and in many others, with such different themes as bread-making, dancing, farming and fighting.

Etruscan artists painted their people with long pointed faces and fully developed bodies. Each figure in this scene has an elegance which is most appealing. Because the artist drew them well and shaded their forms, they appear real as they move briskly along the wall.

Musicians (470 B.C.), Etruscan; Tomb of the Leopards, Tarquinia.

When the mighty Romans conquered Greece, they adopted certain portions of Greek culture while rejecting others. The Romans did not believe in the educational powers of music as did the Greeks. Therefore, less stress was placed upon this aspect of music in their society. Cicero, Roman statesman, orator and author, declared that music could only be of limited service to man. Because of this attitude, the development of new musical instruments was slow in Rome. Music was used primarily in connection with military life. In the category of military music, the Romans surpassed the Greeks.

Stringed instruments were rare among the Romans. Those which were used were borrowed from other countries, but improved upon. One instrument which Romans helped to develop more than any other was the *hydraulis,* or water organ. It was the most important musical instrument in Rome. The Emperor Nero had this instrument at his court. The water organ was also used in the amphitheatre, where it accompanied the contests of the gladiators. Musical sounds came from the instrument whenever water was poured into, or released from, a column in the instrument's air chamber.

This Roman fresco was done less than a century before the birth of Christ. The gracious figures, a lady playing a *cithera,* one of the rare stringed instruments of Rome, and a young girl, who might be her daughter, are about life-size. Both figures have the perfect kind of beauty found in Greek art, but as is typical of Roman art, they seem more lifelike. The painter carefully shaded areas to make them appear more real. He painted his models exactly as they appeared to him. Notice the lady's face, with its fullness, strong nose and piercing eyes. This seems to be a portrait of a specific Roman woman rather than a generalized study of some average lady of the time.

Lady Musician and Young Girl (c. 100 B.C.), Roman; The Metropolitan Museum of Art, New York, Rogers Fund.

The Middle Ages

During the early medieval period there were very few towns left in Europe. Those which remained from the great Roman Empire were practically deserted. New ones were founded, but they were both small and little known. For the most part, people lived in the country and worked on farms owned by rich nobles or monasteries.

By 1100 A.D. towns began to grow again. Many people left farms to find work in the villages, towns and cities which were beginning to cover Europe. These people brought important skills with them. It was just a matter of time before the new towns became centers of wealth, learning and art.

Living in cities was an interesting experience for the people of the Middle Ages. Since they lived so closely together they learned how important it was to cooperate. They also began to think differently about life—especially life in heaven or hell.

A magnificent art style grew out of this change of thinking. It is called the *Gothic* style and it started in France about 1150. From France the new style spread throughout Europe. One of the most glorious forms to come out of Gothic art was the high, slender cathedral with stained glass windows.

Chartres Cathedral is the most beautiful of all Gothic churches. Our figure of *Music* is but one of hundreds of different carvings cut into the Cathedral's walls and doorways. Some of these statues are only a few inches tall while others are life size.

Cathedrals were the most important buildings in the Middle Ages. All of the townspeople helped to build them. Some of these buildings took as long as 300 years to construct. But time didn't matter too much in those days. The thought of making a beautiful house for God was more important.

The unknown sculptor, who carved this image of *Music* on one of the entrances of Chartres Cathedral, made the figure come to life for his townspeople. She seems to move as she hammers away at the bell. Her body is defined by the flow of her garment. With her throne, lyre and bells, she is clearly the symbol and soul of music.

The bells in this relief are common for the period. They are cup-shaped and shallow, with a clapper. Their shape is like that of a beehive. Their tone is weak and whimpering, not the great booming sound we associate with the larger type of bell found in church steeples.

Music (c. 1215-1220), from Chartres Cathedral; Chartres, France, Photograph Giraudon.

The importance of music in the Middle Ages can be seen in this page from a book. Lovely maidens are playing a variety of instruments. They may be performing in the castle yard for the benefit of weary knights who have just returned from battle. They could be playing a concert for the royal family. Whatever the event, their sweet music must have been thoroughly enjoyed.

The maiden on the left is holding a *portative organ.* This was the favorite instrument of the Middle Ages. The portative organ had a clear, pure mellow tone. Because of its keyboard mechanism, it was easy to play. Eventually, this portative organ became the piano accordion we know today.

The *dulcimer,* shown twice in this picture, was also popular in the Middle Ages. It consists of a wooden soundbox across which strings are stretched. Other instruments in the picture are a lute, flute, pommern, recorder and trumpet.

Musicians Playing (15th Century), French; City Library, Grenoble, France.

This charming page illustrating the month of May comes from a combination prayer book and calendar. The famous book from which it is taken is known as *Les Trésriches Heures,* or *The Very Rich Book of Hours.* This book was made for the Duke of Berry by Flemish artists Pol de Limbourg and his two brothers. Duke Berry was an art patron and brother of the king of France.

Although the book contains many handsome pages, the pages showing the months of the year are extraordinary. In these, the artists continue a custom of the Middle Ages — to render the changing occupations and pastimes of the months. Our page of May represents the annual spring festival of *courtiers,* or members of a royal court. They ride through a wood to welcome in the new spring season. Trumpeteers blow heartily into their instruments as they lead the way. Anyone who played for royalty had to be an outstanding musician. He had to know how to play eight other instruments besides the trumpet.

No doubt Pol de Limbourg and his two brothers enjoyed painting the pretty girls with their elegant dresses, the proud horses, the many trees, and the vast castle in the background. There are so many details in this very small scene that it is quite possible the artists had to use a magnifying glass in order to paint all of them.

Month of May, from The Very Rich Book of Hours (c. 1415)
by the de Limbourg Brothers (Active 1402-1416);
Musée de Condé, Chantilly, France, Photograph Giraudon.

Christ Glorified in the Court of Heaven is one of five panels which were part of an altarpiece for the convent of San Domenico in Florence, Italy. The mood of this panel is both pious and gay. Cheerful angels sing and play their instruments as they move across the sky. Christ is being praised by them.

Fra Angelico's great tribute to Christ has the design quality of the art produced during the Middle Ages, although it is a work of the 15th century. It is flat and strongly patterned. At the same time, it does have traces of perspective and sculptured form. These were discoveries of the Italian Renaissance which help make figures appear as though they are real and stand in real space.

Fra Angelico was a monk of the Dominican order. Throughout his life he served the Church by painting the beauty of Christian stories on the walls and altars of churches, monasteries and convents. These paintings are always sweet and gentle in mood. They are filled with beautiful faces, live expressions and delicate colors.

Fra Angelico was the artist's nickname. It means angelic Brother, and was given to him by his fellow monks.

When describing the artist, the noted biographer Vasari wrote:

> "It was his custom never to retouch or repaint any of his works, but to leave them always just as they were when finished the first time; for he believed as he himself said, that such was the will of God. It is said, indeed, that Fra Giovanni (Angelico) never took a brush in his hand until he had first offered a prayer; nor did he paint a Crucifixion without tears streaming down his cheeks. And both in the faces and attitudes of his figures it is easy to find proof of his sincere and deep devotion to the religion of Christ."

Detail, Christ Glorified in the Court of Heaven (1435) by Fra Angelico (1387-1455); National Gallery, London.

Angels, details from Altarpiece (c. 1490) by Hans Memling (1430-1494); Antwerp Museum, Belgium.

Fifteenth century painting was almost always inspired by religion, and angels playing music was a frequently chosen subject. One of the great works of this period is an altarpiece by the Flemish master Hans Memling (Memlick) depicting angelic musicians performing on instruments of the day.

Paintings such as this let us study the musical instruments of medieval Flanders. The angel on the far left plays a zither, the next one a trumscheit (trom-shyt), the third one a lute, the fourth angel a shawm, and the fifth one a trumpet. The *zither* came to Europe from the Near East. In fact, nearly all musical instruments of medieval Europe came from Asia. The zither consists of a flat wooden soundbox over which 27 to 45 strings may be stretched. Four or five melody strings, placed over a fretted finger board, are plucked with a metal ring worn on the right thumb. The remaining strings are plucked with the bare fingers and are used for accompaniment.

The origin and history of the *trumscheit* are almost unknown. At first, this instrument had only one string and was played with the lower end resting on the ground. Later, other strings were added and it was held, as our angel holds it, high in the air at an angle. The strings, when touched lightly with the short bow, produce a pleasant sound.

There were two kinds of *lutes* in the Middle Ages. The first was a long lute having a slender neck two or three times as long as the body. The second type, shown in this example, is the short lute. This lute is narrow, pear-shaped and tapers to the upper end without a distinct neck. Its pegbox is often bent back at an angle to help withstand the pull of the strings, which are strung in pairs.

The *shawm,* predecessor of the oboe, was a

double-reed instrument with fingerholes. The reed mouthpiece had to be taken right into the mouth in order to produce sound. The shawm's tone was shrill and nasal.

The instrument being played at the extreme right is often referred to as an *angel's trumpet,* and with good reason. Several altarpieces have as many as 50 angels playing this type of trumpet—a straight, slim, metal tube with a bell-shaped end.

In the second detail from the altarpiece, the first angel on the far left blows into a longer, more slender angel's trumpet. The next member of this heavenly orchestra plays a shawm. The third member plays a portative organ. This is an instrument we have discussed earlier. In the example here we can easily see the instrument's parts. Notice the keyboard being played with the right hand, the bellows being played with the left hand, and

the 32 pipes which send out the instrument's sound.

A *Gothic harp* is being played by the fourth angel. Clouds hide the lower section of the instrument which rests between the angel's feet. Medieval harps ranged from small to very large. Some could be carried while others were too large to move. Therefore, they had to be played in a stationary position. Some harps had only seven strings while others had as many as 25. During the Middle Ages the harp was a prized instrument that only members of the royal families and aristocracy were permitted to play.

The angel on the extreme right plays a *medieval fiddle,* the major bowed instrument of Europe in the Middle Ages. The earliest paintings of European fiddles in the tenth century show instruments with one, three, four, and five strings. Five strings became the favored number for the medieval fiddle.

Mary, Queen of Heaven (c. 1480-1489) by the Master of the Saint Lucy Legend (Active 1480-1489); National Gallery of Art, Washington, D. C. Samuel H. Kress Collection.

The unknown artist of this painting is called the Master of the Saint Lucy Legend because his work was very similar to a painting of Saint Lucy in the church of Saint Jacques in Bruges, Belgium. Many scholars believe he was Flemish. *Mary, Queen of Heaven* was probably painted in Flanders. The buildings and countryside in it are typical of that region.

Mary is being taken into paradise on a crescent moon. She was a major symbol of the Church during the Middle Ages, and is often shown standing on the moon. Because of her importance during this period of history, many works of art were dedicated to her glory. In addition to large magnificent paintings such as this one, great cathedrals were created for her.

The title of our painting comes from the holy hymn, *Hail, Queen of Heaven,* being sung by the choir of angels. Their voices are enriched with beautiful music. Angels play dulcimers, harps, lutes, shawms and other instruments of the Middle Ages.

The rich variety of musical instruments shown in this work reflects the advanced stage of music at this period. Flanders contributed greatly to its development.

The Renaissance

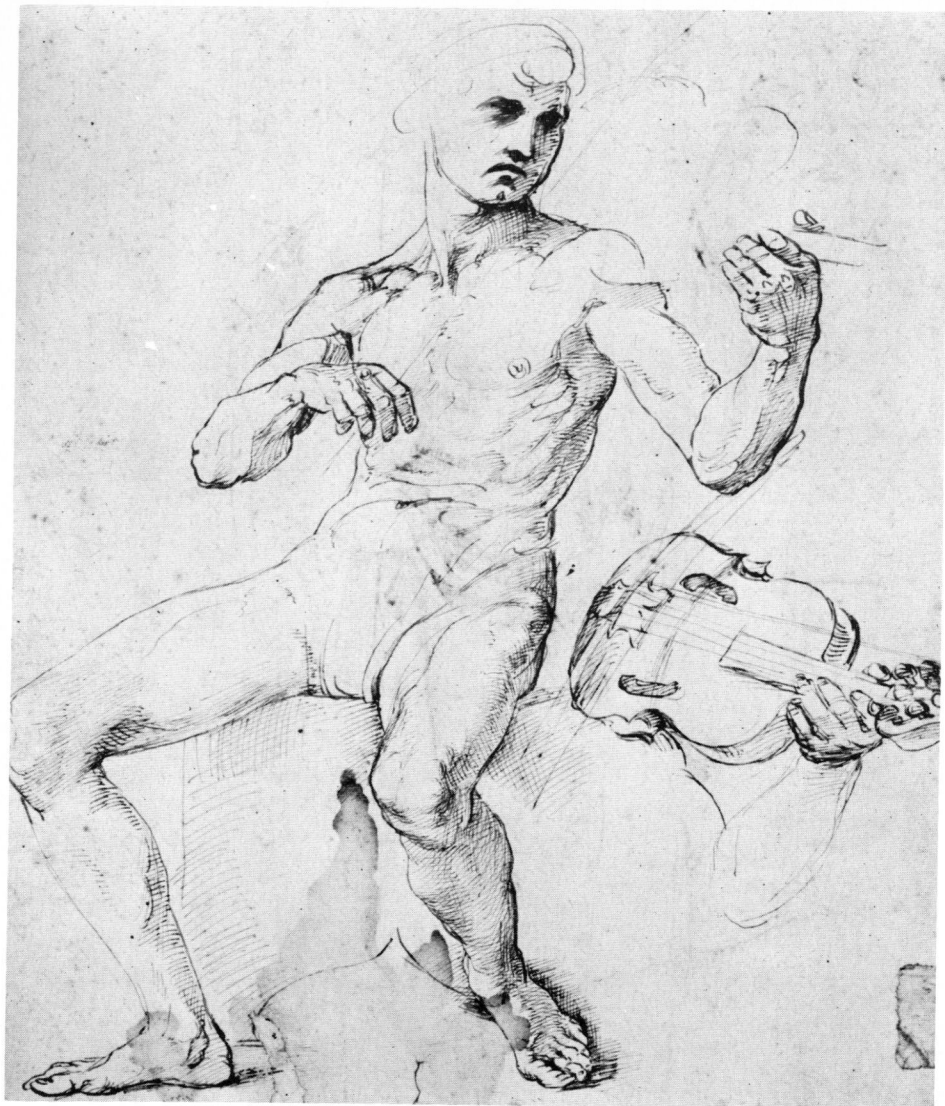

Apollo, study for Parnassus by Raphael; Musée Wicar, Lille, France.

During the *Renaissance,* the period of new learning in Europe between medieval and modern times, musical instruments were used as symbols in paintings. They were meant to stand for various ideas. In most cases, the instruments were associated with special people from legends and history.

In both Raphael's sketch, and finished work, of Apollo, Greek god of youth, beauty, poetry and music, we find him holding a violin. According to legend, the violin represents divine power. Therefore, since Apollo was a divine being, or a god, in Greek thought, he is often shown playing the symbolic violin.

The sketch of Apollo is probably one of many made by the artist for the final fresco called *Parnassus,* a sacred mountain where pagan gods lived. Notice the slight differences between the initial sketch and the completed figure of Apollo. It is common for an artist to make changes as he works. Which of the two do you like best?

Apollo, detail from Parnassus by Raphael (1483-1520); Vatican, Rome, Alinari-Art Reference Bureau.

Raphael's father was also a painter. But he was not as talented as his son. After a period of study with an accomplished painter named Perugino, the young Raphael left his home and traveled to Florence, the center of the Renaissance. While he was in this magnificent city he studied the paintings and sculptures of Leonardo da Vinci and Michelangelo, two geniuses of the Renaissance. He discovered qualities in their works which helped him develop his own style of painting. At the age of 25 Raphael was good enough to compete with da Vinci and Michelangelo. He was called to Rome to design and execute frescos for the Vatican Palace. *Parnassus* was one of these important works.

Because Raphael was an outstanding painter, he was always in demand. The most influential art patrons of the time clamored for his services. He died at the early age of 37 and was buried with honors in the ancient Pantheon, Italy's resting place for its great men.

Saint Cecilia, detail of the Ghent Altarpiece (c. 1432 A.D.) by Hubert (1366-1426) and Jan (1385-1441) Van Eyck; St. Bavon, Ghent, Belgium.

Legend tells us that Saint Cecilia is the patron saint of music. The story of her life and death was a favorite theme for artists of the Renaissance. She is believed to have lived sometime in the third century A.D. Of noble Roman birth, Saint Cecilia was remarkably holy, and composed sweet hymns which brought the angels from heaven to listen as she sang. According to the story, the saint could not find a suitable instrument to express her love for God; therefore, she invented the organ.

Apparently, Saint Cecilia made a vow to devote her life and divine voice to the glory of God. During the process of keeping this pledge she was captured, along with her husband and an angel. Both Cecilia and her husband, a converted pagan, were sentenced to death for converting pagans to Christianity.

The saint's husband was the first to be executed. Next, they threw Saint Cecilia into a bath of boiling water, but she emerged as refreshed as from a cool lagoon. Finally, she was killed, but lived long enough to give her wealth to the poor. She died with a hymn of praise for God on her lips.

This is a detail from the *Ghent Altarpiece* by the Van Eyck (van-ik) brothers, Hubert and Jan. Jan Van Eyck, the younger of the two brothers, is credited with the invention of oil painting, the media used in this work. The entire *Ghent Altarpiece* includes 12 panels and measures 11 x 14 feet. It illustrates their version of the legend. They have painted the saint in deep meditation, perhaps composing a song for God, as she strokes the keys of the organ.

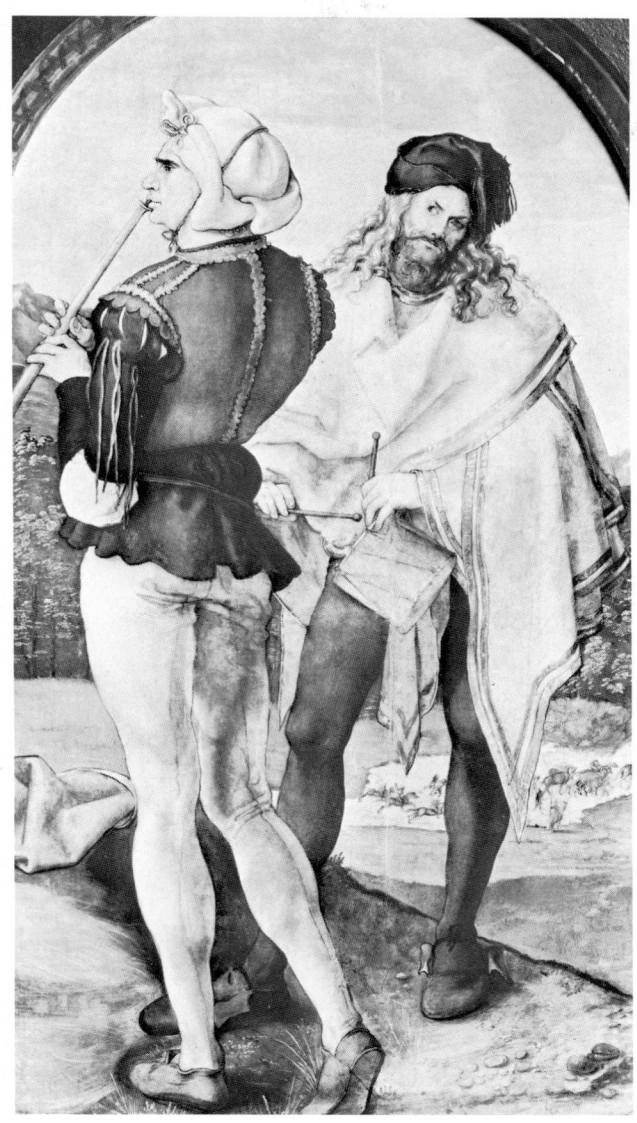

Piper and Drummer, Verso of a wing of the Three Kings Altar (1504) by Albrecht Dürer (1471-1528); Wallraf-Richartz Museum, Cologne.

These skeptical looking musicians are doing their part in the drama of the degradation of Job being played out in the *Three Kings Altar* by Albrecht Dürer. The central panel shows Job on the dunghill with his wife pouring slops over him, as told in the Bible. In our example, the piper and drummer are mocking Job, although Job is not pictured.

Drums are still used in this respect today, especially by the armed forces whenever one of their number is dishonorably discharged. He is "drummed out," as the saying goes.

Does the drum in this painting seem unusually small? It is a type of the snare, a drum with snares of gut or wire stretched across the lower head, which produces a dry, rattling tone. Generally, the *snare drum* consists of a wooden or metal shell and two drummer heads, which are attached to the shell by rods. Sound is achieved by beating the drummer heads with a pair of drumsticks made of wood.

As a child, Dürer revealed exceptional drawing talent. The high quality of his early work enabled him to become an apprentice with the most important workshop in Nuremberg, Germany, where he excelled in making altarpieces and woodcut illustrations. After serving his apprenticeship, the young artist followed the custom of the times and traveled to broaden his experience and to find a place to set up a studio. Fortunately for Nuremberg, Dürer returned to settle there. He became one of Germany's greatest masters. Even Emperor Maximilian, the Holy Roman Emperor, sought his services.

Whenever the artist visited the Netherlands, he was received like a lord. The painters of Antwerp even honored him with a magnificent banquet. Later, Dürer described the event in these terms: "and when I was led to the table, the people stood, on both sides, as if they were introducing a lord, and among them were many persons of excellence who all bowed their heads in the most humble manner."

An Orchestra of Venetian Painters, from the Marriage of Cana (1563) by Paolo Veronese (1528-1588); Louvre, Paris, Photograph Giraudon.

Have you found the artist in this group? Paolo Veronese (ve-ro-NA-ze) is located on the left, and is playing a violoncello. Other masters in the painting include Titian playing the double-bass, Tintoretto the viola, and Bassano the flute. In this beautifully composed group of musicians, all of whom were very famous Venetian artists, Veronese has given us a clear idea of the importance of music in Venetian artistic life and in the life of the general public as well.

During Veronese's day, it was customary for rich chapters of monks, who were in charge of the elaborate Venetian churches, to com-mission artists to decorate the walls of their dining halls with scenes of feasts from the Old or New Testament. Veronese was chosen to paint four such Biblical banquets. This is a detail from one of these fresco masterpieces, *Marriage at Cana.*

Veronese carefully arranged his subjects to present them at different levels. The textures of objects are brought out by the play of light on figures and instruments. He, like other Venetian masters, attempted to capture light's special qualities. Perhaps this is natural because his surroundings in Venice, the city of canals, were constantly bathed in golden light.

Saint Cecilia and an Angel (c. 1610) by Orazio Gentileschi (c. 1565-1640); National Gallery of Art, Washington, D. C., Samuel H. Kress Collection.

Orazio Gentileschi (gent-i-LES-key) painted Cecilia, the patron saint of music, some 200 years after Jan and Hubert Van Eyck painted the *Ghent Altarpiece.* His choice of Saint Cecilia as a subject for a painting shows the continuing interest in her legend.

Gentileschi's saint is dressed in the costume of the time in which the painting was made, and wears her hair in the fashion of the day. She seems to be a very pleasant, ordinary person deeply involved in her music making.

The strong lights and darks in this picture are common to the painting of the period. Both the saint and the angel are spotlighted against a dark background. They glow in this light, which brings out their pretty, gentle, almost childlike faces. Perhaps more than anything else, Gentileschi is known for the tender quality of his paintings.

Pieter Brueghel (BREW-gul) is remembered for his scenes of peasant life. He was considered the cleverest Dutch painter of the 16th century. The majority of his works combine both country life and landscape, as can be seen in *The Wedding Dance*.

Dancing, talking, eating, and drinking, these rather plain looking people seem to be enjoying themselves on this festive occasion. Brueghel has painted his country folk in bright, flat colors and has reduced shadows to a minimum. Nevertheless, the bodies seem solid. The figures and trees have been placed carefully to give the painting a sense of deep space. We can almost hear the sound of the bagpipe, the voices of the peasants, and the stomping of feet, in this merry scene.

The bagpipe is one of the most common instruments in Brueghel's folk paintings. Throughout Europe bagpipes were popular as folk instruments, since they were made by hand and played by country people. As such, they are still used today, and have survived in Scotland and Ireland as military instruments. Bagpipes came to Europe from Asia about the first century A.D.

The Wedding Dance by Pieter Brueghel the Elder (1525/30-1569); Courtesy, Detroit Institute of Arts.

Another Dutch artist interested in painting pictures of the peasant was Adriane Van Ostade (OSS-tad). The son of a weaver, Van Ostade became one of the most important painters of Dutch everyday life.

In *The Golden Wedding*, a happy occasion is being celebrated. The fiddler's music seems to have brought joy and a good time into their lives. The dancers bow to each other and the people listen and gossip as the fiddler saws away. He may be a wandering music-maker, or a friendly neighbor. Notice the several stunted people around the room. Little people can be found in many of Van Ostade's paintings.

Genre (ZHAN-ruh), or scenes of everyday life, occupies an important place in 17th century Dutch paintings. Van Ostade belongs to a group of painters often referred to as "Little Masters," because they painted cozy interiors and landscapes associated with the love of home and pride in their country. The works of these painters were bought by average citizens, who hung them proudly in their simple homes.

The Golden Wedding (1674) by Adriane Van Ostade (1610-1685); The Art Institute of Chicago, George B. and Mary R. Harris Fund.

The Music Lesson (c. 1660) by Gerard Terborch (1617-1681); The Art Institute of Chicago, Gift of Charles T. Yerkes.

The Concert by Gerard Terborch; Dahlem Museum, Berlin.

In *The Music Lesson,* Gerard Terborch (Ter-BOORKH) paints an entirely different type scene than his countryman Van Ostade. The son of a tax-collector, Terborch belonged to a higher level of society and accordingly painted the upper classes. He was a master at rendering the textures of silks, satins and velvets worn by his well-to-do sitters, and was unrivaled in painting fabrics realistically.

The Concert is considered one of Terborch's finest works, although there is some question about whether he painted the woman sitting behind the harpsichord. She appears to be uncomfortable in her corner and might have been added by a lesser artist sometime after Terborch finished the canvas. The masterly treatment of the principal figure, shown from the back, makes up for the weaker figure in the corner.

There is a good possibility that the *harpsichord* shown in this painting was made in Italy. Italy was the center of harpsichord production in the 16th and 17th centuries. At this time the instrument reached the height of its popularity, which lasted until the next century. The modern piano, as we know it today, came into prominence in the 18th century, replacing the harpsichord as the number one keyboard instrument.

Mezzetin by Jean-Antoine Watteau; The Metropolitan Museum of Art, New York, Munsey Fund.

Antoine Watteau's (va-toe) art records the period in French history when the aristocracy, or the "upper crust," ruled supreme. They enjoyed countless festivals and pageants. Watteau's paintings of their gay picnics in lush park settings, and musical parties where all the guests are handsome and beautifully dressed, are truly dream-like. The works of Watteau depict the world of pleasure, of the theatre, music and dance. They show, in a very pleasing way, the taste of French court society in the early 18th century. The name given to the art of this time is *Rococo;* a style of soft pastel colors and pretty decoration.

One of the Watteau's favorite subjects was an actor of the time. His canvas, *Mezzetin,* shows the actor playing a guitar. We can also study Watteau's preliminary sketch for the finished painting. He, too, made changes, as did Raphael in the latter's studies for his fresco *Parnassus.* But Watteau's differences are not as great. Do you see how he has slightly altered the position of the actor's legs and the angle of his head?

The guitar in this scene is an Italian model. The actor was probably one of the many Italians who performed regularly in France. These players were so admired by French society that their favorite instrument, the guitar, became very popular. A number of Watteau's paintings show elegantly dressed ladies playing an Italian version of the guitar.

Watteau's paintings are filled with happiness. But he was not a happy person. On the contrary, the artist suffered extreme hardships throughout his life. Shortly after reaching fame and fortune, he contacted a deadly disease which made it difficult for him to paint. We are fortunate that this rare genius, who died at the age of 37, lived long enough to paint the beauty of his times.

Studies of a Guitar Player by Jean-Antoine Watteau (1648-1721); British Museum, London.

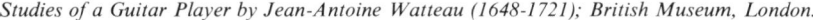

The Modern World

Although musical instruments have always appeared in art, it is in the work of the 19th and 20th centuries that they have truly reached their peak. Practically all modern French masters, and many American artists, include instruments in their works. Stringed instruments, because of their great variety, are the most popular.

Ten thousand dollars is a sizable amount of money to pay for a painting, even today. However, the American painter William M. Harnett received this much, and even more, for his fantastically realistic still lifes, almost one hundred years ago. The public and critics alike were amazed by his ability to paint objects convincing enough to make one want to lift them from the canvas' surface.

Old Models is but one of several of these gems executed by Harnett. The bugle, a military type, and the violin in this painting seem to be the artist's favorite musical motifs. This type of bugle was originally a hunter's horn, but it became a military instrument at the end of the 18th century when battle formation became too large for shouted commands to be heard.

Harnett builds his composition around the bugle and violin in the same way that an architect constructs the framework of a building. This rigid arrangement of forms can be easily overlooked because the painting's unbelievable detail attracts our attention first.

The painted objects look so real in Harnett's still lifes that many viewers reach for them. During an industrial display in Cincinnati, a painting entitled *The Violin* so tempted spectators to try to take down the hanging bow and fiddle that officials had to stand near the painting to discourage this notion. The artist must have been very happy when he learned of this incident.

William Harnett was trained as an *engraver*, one who cuts designs on wood or metal for reproduction, before he began painting. We can guess safely that he developed a fondness for fine detail from the demands made on him by his engraver's craft.

Old Models (c. 1890-1892) by William M. Harnett (1848-1892); Courtesy, Museum of Fine Art, Boston.

Thomas Eakins, one of America's greatest artists, was a contemporary of William Harnett. There is a special warmth about Eakins' *Musicians Rehearsing.* Music was an important part of his life, and he shared it with others through his paintings on musical themes.

Eakins had a life-long interest in the beauty of bone and muscle, one which took hold in his early years as a student at the Jefferson Medical School, where he studied *anatomy,* the science of the body's structure. Eakins' main purpose there was "to increase my knowledge of how beautiful objects are put together" in order to imitate them with great accuracy.

In addition to anatomy, photography interested the artist. He was concerned mainly about the relationship between photography and the way we see objects, whether they be water, sky, people, or small objects. Eakins often photographed a scene which appealed to him, studied it carefully, and then painted the scene using the photograph as a source of information.

The Banjo Lesson (c. 1875) by Henry O. Tanner;
Hampton Institute, Hampton, Virginia.

This tender painting by Henry O. Tanner, a student of Thomas Eakins, is a document of his teacher's philosophy. Eakins summed it up in these words:

> "If America is to produce painters and if young art students wish to assume a place in the history of art of their country, their first desire should be to remain in America, and to peer into the heart of American life."

The Banjo Lesson is, indeed, a penetrating view into a segment of American life. It reveals the same sense of gentle sadness found in everyday scenes by the older Eakins. But Tanner, the son of a Methodist bishop, did not follow his master's advice about staying in America. He left in his early thirties to paint in Europe, where his works would be judged on artistic merit alone, without the brand of having been produced by a Negro.

The Sleeping Gypsy (1897) by Henri Rousseau (1844-1910); Collection, The Museum of Modern Art, New York.

A year after Henry Rousseau (roo-so) paint-ed *The Sleeping Gypsy* he wrote the following letter to the mayor of his home town, Laval, France:

> "I have the honor of sending you these few lines as a native of your town, who has become a self-taught artist and is desirous that his native city possess one of his works, pro-posing that you purchase from me a genre painting entitled *The Sleep-ing Gypsy,* which measures 2m. 60 in width and 1m. 90 in height. A wandering Negress, who plays the mandolin, with her jar next to her (a vase containing drinking water), is deeply asleep, worn out from fa-tigue. A lion happens to go by, sniffs at her, and does not devour her. There is an effect of moonlight, very poetic. The scene takes place in a completely arid desert. The gypsy is dressed in oriental fashion.
>
> I will let it go for 2,000 or 1,800 francs, for I would be happy to let the town of Laval possess a remem-brance of one of its children."

Unfortunately, for Rousseau, the offer was rejected, but fortunately for us the painting is in an American museum.

During the artist's lifetime gypsy stories were popular in France. He probably based this painting on such a story. Lions were often part of a traveling gypsy carnival. Rousseau added an instrument because gypsies earned their living by playing music in carnivals.

Rousseau was the son of a humble trades-man. At 18 he volunteered for the army and served in Mexico. On his return he became a minor customs official, hence the name *Douanier* by which he is also known. At the age of 40, he retired to become a full-time painter. Some of his earliest works are copies of picture postcards, paintings of park set-tings, and portraits of family members and friends, usually taken from photographs. He received only a small pension and lived poorly. His studio consisted of only a table, three chairs, a chest and a bed behind a cur-tain. His meals were bread soaked in milk or wine. Rousseau lived a simple life and died a pauper. Today his paintings are very valu-able.

*Musicians (1872) by Edgar Degas (1834-1917);
Städelsches Kunstinstitut, Frankfort.*

Edgar Degas (duh-GAH) captured the impression of quick action in his painting *Musicians.* Like Eakins he was impressed with the art of photography. Degas developed a new way of arranging objects in paintings based on photographic principles, like the unexpected angle and the close-up view. When we look at this canvas, our eye moves from the members of the orchestra in the foreground to the small ballet dancers in the background. A vast sense of space is suggested by this arrangement. Photographers use a similar technique whenever they frame pictures with foreground objects.

Another influence on Degas, and other artists working in Paris during the second half of the 19th century, was the Japanese print. These were used as wrappings and paddings for china imported from Japan, and could be found easily in Parisian tea-shops. Degas collected the prints and studied them to learn new ways of composing paintings. He liked the off-center compositions and strong outlines used by Japanese artists.

Ballet was one of Degas' favorite themes. At rehearsals he could study numerous poses taken by dancers, as well as experiment with unusual vantage points from high above the stage. Intricate foreshortening and the strange effects of stage-lighting on the dancers' bodies concerned him most. He also was intrigued by the interplay of light and shade on human forms. Although casual in appearance, *Musicians* is composed with great care. Degas was a master of design and drawing.

Side Show (1887-1888) by Georges Seurat (1859-1891); The Metropolitan Museum of Art, New York, Bequest of Stephen C. Clark.

Georges Seurat was groping with the problem of representing figures out-of-doors when he painted *Side Show.* Those flower-like shapes along the top of the paintings are flaring jets of gas. Before attempting this canvas, Seurat sketched a number of parades. Each of these sketches reveal a careful study of the play of light on form.

Attention is drawn to this particular show by cornet players wearing derbies and a clown playing the trombone. The mustached man on the right, the showman, waits for the cue before launching into his part of the act. He also serves as a device to keep our eye from going outside the picture plane and to help us focus on the most prominent figure in the painting—the clown. Notice how the figures appear either in profile or front views, and how they are fitted into a system of horizontal and vertical bands.

One of the most systematic painters of all times, Seurat was the founder of *pointillism,* the method he used to construct this painting. The artist applied small separated spots, or dots of pure color, side by side on his canvas. At a distance the eye is supposed to mix the color dots in order to make more colors than there are in the painting.

This strange, assorted collection of vagabonds, thought to be Polish refugees who lived near the artist's studio in Paris, represents one of Edouard Manet's most striking early works. *The Old Musician* was completed in the artist's 30th year.

When this canvas was being painted, a group of young French artists were revolting against officials who controlled admission to important exhibitions called "Salons." These artists wanted to paint objects as they saw them— warmly, truthfully, and scientifically. Among this group was Manet. He was openly opposed to the smooth, photographic surface admired by the public and critics.

Instead, Manet treated his themes in a sketchy and informal manner. This attitude can be seen easily in *The Old Musician.* Forms are flat and almost in silhouette, two radical departures from the accepted way of painting. The artist reduced shadow in order to display strong brushwork, as in the shirt of the boy with the straw hat.

Critics raged about Manet's unorthodox style. However, it encouraged other artists to experiment with new ways of seeing objects. In *The Old Musician,* Manet's brush stroking is quick and precise. His fluid manner of applying paint was essential to the fleeting effect which formed the basis for

Impressionism. This movement began in France in the 1860's and is usually considered to be the beginning of modern art. It attempted to capture impressions of nature, not photographic copies.

Four years after he painted *The Old Musician,* Manet painted *The Fifer* pictured on page 54. The gaily uniformed young boy seems to be blowing without effort into his fife. The instrument has him under its spell. Notice the flat poster-like quality of this painting. Yet, the fifer appears real and solid even though the colors are flat, the shadows are few, and the shading is at a minimum.

How does the artist achieve this effect? Manet used separate patches of pure color instead of shaded colors. Second, he placed these patches of color next to each other with no overlappings. Third, he gave each color patch its own shape, such as the fifer's sash, parts of his uniform, and the instrument. The colors chosen by Manet and the way they are arranged account for the three-dimensional quality of the painting.

Ever since the end of the Middle Ages artists used modeling and shading devices to make objects or people appear solid in their paintings. But, Manet thought form could be developed through differences in color alone, especially flat color. He has proven his ideas.

The Old Musician (1862) by Edouard Manet (1832-1833); National Gallery of Art, Washington, D. C., Dale Collection.

The Fifer (1866) by Edouard Manet; Louvre, Paris.

Detail, Two Girls at the Piano (1892) by Auguste Renoir (1841-1918); Louvre, Paris.

Auguste Renoir is one of the most popular of the Impressionists. As a youngster he was apprenticed to a porcelain decorator. For hours the young artist painted flowers and other motifs onto the cups and plates. The delicacy of technique and the love of fresh blues, greens and pinks which developed from this apprenticeship tinged Renoir's style throughout his life.

The delightful young girls at the piano are engrossed in their music. Light falls gently on their faces, hair, dresses and other objects in the room. It holds the composition together and gives it great warmth. This painting employs one of Renoir's favorite devices —a pair of figures, one standing in the background encircling a seated foreground figure.

The soft edges and lack of detail in *Two Girls at the Piano* may be due partially to an illness Renoir suffered three years before this canvas was painted. The pain was so severe that, in order to continue painting, he had to sit in a wheelchair with his brush strapped to his hand. Once a visitor asked the artist how he was able to paint under these circumstances. Renoir answered, "One does not paint with one's hands." Perhaps he was hoping to tell his visitor that for him painting came from the heart.

57

The Old Guitarist (1903) by Pablo Picasso (1881-   ); The Art Institute of Chicago, Helen Birch Bartlett Memorial Collection.

A young Spanish artist arrived in Paris in the year 1900. He was unknown, poor, and desperately lonely for his family and friends. *The Old Guitarist* was painted during this period of despair. In the blue color, the color of gloomy things, this starved musician looks very sad. Pablo Picasso's unhappiness during the early years of his career is reflected in this painting and others painted at the same time which also have blue as the dominant color. These works are commonly referred to as paintings of the artist's *Blue Period.*

From those humble beginnings, Picasso has become the most remarkable and influential artist of our century. According to many scholars, he is the painter who most completely represents the quality of our modern world. He was born in Malaga, Spain. When his family moved to Barcelona in 1896, Picasso entered the Academy of Fine Arts. In one day he completed an entrance examination for which a month was usually allowed. He repeated this performance soon afterwards in Madrid. At the age of 16, when most artists are still in the process of learning basics, Picasso had his first exhibition. What happened afterwards—his early years in Paris as co-founder of *Cubism,* his skill in painting, sculpture, graphics, and ceramics —is almost legend.

These two paintings by Picasso were made 18 years after *The Old Guitarist* we discussed earlier. His style had changed considerably. The similarity of the two paintings done in the same year show how an artist often pushes and explores one idea. It is interesting to compare these works. The artist has used pieces of colored shapes which fit together like a puzzle. In each painting the pieces make three masked people in costumes. They are Harlequin, Pierrot, and a monk. Each figure has a musical instrument which he plays with apparent glee. Can you find them and their instruments?

Both *Three Musicians* are good examples of *Cubism,* a style developed by Picasso and Georges Braque (brock). Space is flattened out in the works of this style. For example, although the trios in our paintings are supposed to represent real people they are painted as cardboard cutouts. If our musicians would step out of the painting they would be flat, thin, strange looking creatures. But, as long as they remain in the picture it is not too difficult to think of them as representing regular three-dimensional people even though they are masked and we can not see their faces. The artist has played a trick on our eyes by flattening out space.

Three Musicians (1921) by Pablo Picasso; Collection, The Museum of Modern Art, New York.

Three Musicians (1921) by Pablo Picasso; Philadelphia Museum of Art, A. E. Gallatin Collection.

Violin and Palette (1909-1910) by Georges Braque (1882-1963);
The Solomon R. Guggenheim Museum, New York.

In 1908, Georges Braque started a lifelong series of still lifes. The objects in these paintings were almost always taken from the kitchen cupboard. In addition to food and drink, Braque included tobacco, cards, chessboards, newspapers, books and musical instruments in his still lifes.

Violin and Palette is one of many such paintings. It is one of a series painted by the artist in 1909. Later, when speaking about these paintings Braque said:

> "....I painted a good many musical instruments.... because I was surrounded with them .... The peculiar thing about a musical instrument, as an object, is that you can bring it to life by touching it."

Georges Braque believed that since a painting is a flat surface it should be kept a flat surface, brought to life by line, color, and texture. To bring out this view, Braque began to construct *collages*. These are compositions made by pasting together a number of materials, such as newspaper, wallpaper, cardboard, cloth, and pages from books. All of these items are flat, but they have interesting lines, colors, and textures.

Musical Forms is a collage. It illustrates Braque's interest in using flat forms to preserve the two-dimensional quality of the canvas on which it is painted. Furthermore, the collage's subject matter—musical instruments—reveals the artist's great love of musical themes.

Musical Forms (1918) by Georges Braque (1882-1963); Philadelphia Museum of Art, Arensberg Collection.

The Violin Player by Raoul Dufy (1877-1953); Collection of Dr. Aubert, Nice, France.

Raoul Dufy's (do-fee) art is especially gay, festive, and bright. His water colors and oils sing with life and freshness. There is a special spontaneous simplicity and easiness about Dufy's work. To make things look easy— especially when they are difficult—is a very high achievement.

Dufy was born in Le Havre, France, one of nine children. He and his brother Jean became successful painters and two other brothers became musicians. Music was an important part of their family life. This love for music is very evident as it is a theme which appears over and over in Dufy's art. Dufy listened to musicians in small chamber groups to large symphony orchestras performing and practicing music of all moods. With his fast and selective eye he recreated stimulating evenings of music.

The Quintet with Red Cello (1948) by Raoul Dufy (1877-1953); Private Collection, Paris.

66

*The Green Violinist (1922) by Marc Chagall (1887-   );
The Solomon R. Guggenheim Museum, New York.*

The musician has become part of his instrument in this fairy tale picture. Marc Chagall enjoys the world of make-believe. His paintings often show floating people, dreaming cows, topsy turvy landscapes and flying fish. Where does the artist get his ideas? His vivid imagination and the memories of his childhood in a small Russian village, rich in folklore, are two of the most important sources.

This is an engraving called a *drypoint*. In order to make this engraving, Chagall had to cut lines into a metal plate with a sharp tool called a *burin*. Next, he filled the lines with ink which made the resulting image—a violinist—when paper was pressed against the metal plate. There is a definite advantage to this kind of technique. A large number of pictures can be made from one metal plate. The process is similar to that used to print our daily newspapers.

Marc Chagall

Woman at the Piano (1955) by Philip Evergood (1901-   );
Johnson Wax Collection of Contemporary American Paintings.

This dreamy-eyed singer waits for her cue and accompanist before beginning her song. The ferns in the vase next to her seem to bend in her direction. Perhaps they, too, want to be serenaded and do not want to miss a note.

From the way the artist placed the lines on the floor it is easy to get the impression that the singer and her piano are floating in mid-air. These zig-zag lines are part of the floor as well as part of the wallpaper. In reality they can not be one and the same. Philip Evergood has intentionally made them this way in order to fascinate us with his manipulation of space. Although the space in this picture is somewhat strange to our eye we can still enjoy the painting.

Throughout his life Evergood has painted pictures having both unusual space and subject matter. Most of his works are crowded with people. Some of these show them fighting. Evergood often tries to teach moral lessons through his paintings, which depict violent action and hate.

The artist's father was also a painter. Because Evergood's father did not want him to become a painter, too, he sent him to private schools in England so that the boy would learn another profession. But Evergood was not interested in anything except art. He studied in England with the best painters in the country. When he returned to America he became a success. His paintings are appreciated today for their honesty and technical skill.

97/55   Ben Shahn   Ben Shahn

Silent Music (1951) by Ben Shahn (1898-   );
Philadelphia Museum of Art.

Not all paintings or drawings having musical themes include musicians or instruments. This work by one of America's most important artists, Ben Shahn, shows their empty chairs and music stands. The musicians are gone. The concert has ended. This book has ended. I hope your interest in art and music will never end.

the Author

Dr. Donald D. Celender was born in Pittsburgh, Pennsylvania, and obtained his education in his native city. He received his Bachelor of Fine Arts degree from the Carnegie Institute of Technology and his Master's degree in Education and Doctor of Philosophy degree in Art History from the University of Pittsburgh. Dr. Celender is a teacher, a writer, a lecturer, and a sculptor and painter. His paintings, sculpture and stained glass mosaics have been displayed in numerous exhibitions and one-man shows, and he has been the recipient of several national and regional awards. Dr. Celender has been a lecturer at the National Gallery of Art in Washington and the Director of Education and Public Activities at The Minneapolis Institute of Arts. At present he is Art Historian at Macalester College, St. Paul, Minnesota.